Dig!

Written by
Jill Atkins

You can fill a bucket with so much sand!
You can look for shells in the sand too.

Jack dug in the sand.

He dug up a fossil.
It was next to the cliff, hidden in the sand.

Do you like to dig in the garden?

It is so much fun!

You can dig with a fork in the soil.

You can dig so deep.

This digger will dig deep too.

It will dig a channel with its scoop.

It can lift such a big load.

This is a **rock pipit**.
It will dig in the rocks.

It will look for a snail for its dinner.

Do you like this woodpecker?

It digs into the tree.

It pecks and pecks so it can get a bug for its chicks.

Do puffins like to dig?

Yes, they will dig deep in the soil.

They need a nest so the chicks can be born.

Rabbits like to dig too.

They can dig such a long tunnel.

Do you think this dog will like to dig?

Yes! It is so much fun for him to dig in the garden.

They all like to dig!